OLYMPICS
RECORD BREAKERS

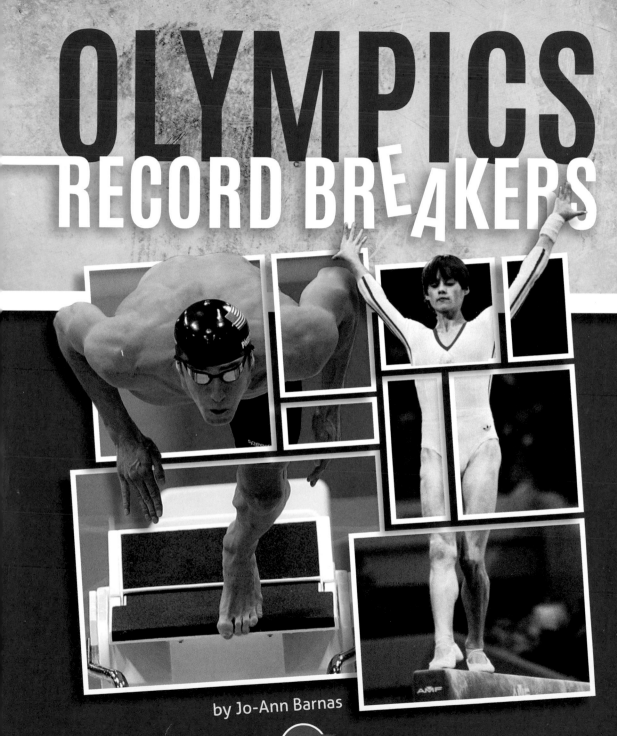

by Jo-Ann Barnas

SportsZone
An Imprint of Abdo Publishing | abdopublishing.com

abdopublishing.com

Published by Abdo Publishing, a division of ABDO, PO Box 398166, Minneapolis, Minnesota 55439. Copyright © 2016 by Abdo Consulting Group, Inc. International copyrights reserved in all countries. No part of this book may be reproduced in any form without written permission from the publisher. SportsZone™ is a trademark and logo of Abdo Publishing.

Printed in the United States of America, North Mankato, Minnesota
042015
092015

Cover Photo: Michael Sohn/AP Images, cover (left); AP Images, cover (right)
Interior Photos: Michael Sohn/AP Images, 1 (left); AP Images, 1 (right), 9, 10; Bettmann/Corbis, 5, 44; Sport the Library SportsChrome/Newscom, 6; Sven Simon/Imago/Icon Sportswire, 13, 18; Werner Schulze/Imago/Icon Sportswire, 15; Magic/Imago/Icon Sportswire, 16; Ed Reinke/AP Images, 21, 26; Katsumi Kasahara/AP Images, 22; Bruno Torres/AP Images, 25; Petr David Josek/AP Images, 29, 34, 38; ZumaPress/Icon Sportswire, 30; Nhat V. Meyer/MCT/Newscom, 33; David J. Phillip/AP Images, 37; Mark J. Terrill/AP Images, 41, 42; Sal J. Veder/AP Images, 45

Editor: Patrick Donnelly
Series Designer: Nikki Farinella

Library of Congress Control Number: 2015931746

Cataloging-in-Publication Data
Barnas, Jo-Ann.
 Olympics record breakers / Jo-Ann Barnas.
  p. cm. -- (Record breakers)
Includes bibliographical references and index.
ISBN 978-1-62403-849-5
1. Olympics--Juvenile literature. 2. Olympics--Records--Juvenile literature.
I. Title.
796.48--dc23

2015931746

TABLE OF CONTENTS

1 Beamon Takes Flight 4

2 A Perfect Performance 12

3 Double-Double Diver 20

4 Brilliance on the Beach 28

5 Making a Splash 36

Fun Facts 44

Glossary 46

For More Information 47

Index 48

About the Author 48

Note: All records in this book are current through 2014.

1
BEAMON
TAKES FLIGHT

The crowd was cheering, but Bob Beamon could still hear his friend's voice.

"Come on! Make it a good one!" yelled Ralph Boston, his teammate on the US Olympic track team at the 1968 Summer Games in Mexico City, Mexico.

Beamon began to sprint down the runway. He did not know it at the time, but with each step he was getting closer to smashing the Olympic record in the long jump.

Bob Beamon, *center*, sports his gold medal atop the victory stand after winning the long jump at the 1968 Summer Games in Mexico City, Mexico.

5

Bob Beamon flies through the air during the long jump competition at the 1968 Summer Olympics.

Although Beamon was a gold-medal favorite, he did not feel like it at the time. He was 22 years old. It was his first Olympics. And he was going up against a stacked field. Boston was competing for the third time. He was the gold medalist in the long jump at the 1960 Olympics in Rome, Italy. Then he won silver at the 1964 Olympics in Tokyo,

Japan. The 1964 gold medalist, Great Britain's Lynn Davies, was also back in 1968. So was Igor Ter-Ovanesyan of the Soviet Union. He had won bronze medals in 1960 and 1964. Plus, Boston and Ter-Ovanesyan shared the world record. Needless to say, the field was loaded.

Meanwhile, Beamon had found himself in trouble during the qualifying rounds. He fouled on his first two jumps. That means he stepped on the foul line at the end of the runway before he jumped. He had just one more chance to reach the event finals. But thanks to Boston's help, Beamon began to feel more confident. Boston told him to back up a few steps and adjust his approach to the sandy pit at the end of the runway.

Beamon made the adjustment. He started his jump earlier and did not touch the foul line. He jumped far enough to advance to the Olympic final.

Rain was threatening as Beamon warmed up for the final. Seventeen jumpers had qualified for the last round. Beamon was fourth to jump.

As he sped down the runway, Beamon thought only about landing a clean jump. He had seen the first three jumpers foul on their first attempts. When Beamon leaped into the air and sailed above the sand pit, he looked like he was flying.

When his heels hit the sand, the stadium crowd exploded with cheers. It took a long time for the result to flash on the scoreboard. Beamon had jumped so far the measuring device could not reach the point where his feet hit the sand. Officials needed to use an old-fashioned steel measuring tape to measure his full leap.

The result: 8.90 meters. Unfamiliar with the metric system, Beamon did not know how to react. Boston finally told him that he had jumped more than 29 feet. Beamon had set a world and Olympic record by soaring 29 feet, 2 1/2 inches. That was almost two feet longer than the previous record.

When he realized what he had done, Beamon collapsed in disbelief. Boston and another athlete had to help him back to his feet.

Beamon took one more attempt and jumped 26 feet, 4 1/2 inches (8.03 m). Confident that he would not top his first jump, he passed on his last four chances.

Beamon grew up in New York City. He was also a good basketball player when he was young. He once said that when he was in elementary school everybody always wanted him to be on their team.

In 1965, during his senior year in high school, Beamon was ranked second in the United States in the long jump. He received a scholarship to the University of Texas-El Paso. Three years later, he would make history.

Between 1901 and 1968, the world record in the long jump had been broken 13 times. Usually the record jump

Bob Beamon, *left,* and Ralph Boston huddle under blankets to stay dry as they watch the remaining jumpers try to break Beamon's new world record.

Sand flies as Bob Beamon hits the pit at the end of his world-record long jump at the 1968 Summer Games.

beat the old one by a couple of inches. In 1935, American Jesse Owens set the world record at 26 feet 8 1/4 inches (8.13 m). Over the next 33 years, the record advanced by only 8 3/4 inches (22 cm). Beamon had topped the existing record by 21 3/4 inches (55 cm). He finished more than two feet ahead of silver medalist Klaus Beer of East Germany.

Boston won the bronze medal—his third medal in three Olympics.

Although it was aided by the high altitude of Mexico City, Beamon's jump was considered the world record. It stood for 23 years. Mike Powell of the United States broke it when he jumped 29 feet, 4 3/8 inches (8.95 m) at the 1991 world championships in Tokyo.

While Beamon no longer holds the world record, his jump remains the Olympic record. It was the perfect leap at the perfect time.

ALL-AROUND AMAZING

MANY EXPERTS CONSIDER JACKIE JOYNER-KERSEE THE BEST FEMALE ATHLETE OF ALL TIME. HER RECORD-BREAKING PERFORMANCE IN THE WOMEN'S HEPTATHLON AT THE 1988 SUMMER OLYMPICS IN SEOUL, SOUTH KOREA, BACKS THAT ARGUMENT.

THE HEPTATHLON IS A SERIES OF SEVEN EVENTS CONTESTED OVER TWO DAYS TO FIND THE BEST ALL-AROUND ATHLETE. COMPETITORS EARN POINTS BASED ON THEIR PERFORMANCE IN EACH EVENT.

IN THE FIRST FOUR EVENTS, JOYNER-KERSEE WON THE 100 HURDLES AND THE 200, TIED FOR FIRST IN THE HIGH JUMP, AND TOOK SECOND IN THE SHOT PUT TO SURGE AHEAD. ON THE SECOND DAY, SHE EXTENDED HER LEAD BY ALMOST 400 POINTS AFTER THE LONG JUMP. BY THEN, EVEN WITH TWO EVENTS REMAINING, IT WAS CLEAR THAT THE OLYMPIC GOLD MEDAL, AND NEW WORLD AND OLYMPIC RECORDS, WOULD BE HERS. JOYNER-KERSEE FINISHED WITH 7,291 POINTS, A TOTAL NOT MATCHED SINCE. AND FIVE DAYS LATER, SHE WON HER SECOND GOLD MEDAL IN THE LONG JUMP.

2 A PERFECT PERFORMANCE

In 1976 Nadia Comăneci taught the world about perfection. The 14-year-old Romanian redefined what was possible when she became the first gymnast to score a perfect 10 on a routine.

Her performance on the first day of the 1976 Summer Olympics in Montreal, Canada, was on the uneven bars. That was Comăneci's best event because it demands excellent upper-body strength, split-second timing, and courage. Comăneci had them all. And she put those skills on display on the bars that day.

Gymnast Nadia Comăneci dazzled the world at the 1976 Summer Games in Montreal, Canada.

The 4-foot-11 gymnast delivered a breathtaking performance, releasing and regrasping the bars with ease. Her form was perfect. She displayed straight body lines in the vertical position throughout her routine. And, of course, she stuck her dismount.

What was surprising, though, was that no one expected it—especially the judges. No one had ever been *perfect* before. When Comăneci's score was displayed, it was met with much confusion. The scoreboard at the Montreal Forum read "1.00"—an impossibly low score.

It turned out the scoreboard was not programmed to display a score of 10.00. The highest it could display was 9.99, because a perfect 10 had never been achieved.

Only when a Swedish judge held up 10 fingers did Comăneci and her coaches understand what happened. The public address announcer explained to the crowd the significance of the strange score—that "1.00" actually meant "10.00"—and soon the audience tuning in on TV found out as well.

But the pigtailed Comăneci was far from finished. She went on to record six more perfect scores on the way to winning three gold medals, a silver, and a bronze in Montreal. While her bars routine stands out, she also won gold in the all-around competition. And she helped Romania win the silver medal in the team competition.

Nadia Comăneci flies high during competition on the uneven bars at the 1976 Summer Games.

It might seem impossible to improve on Comăneci's performance in Montreal. But years later, the legendary gymnast said there was one person who was not particularly impressed with her routines.

"I never felt they were perfect," Comăneci told the *Globe and Mail* of Toronto in a 2012 interview. "They were very good, but I still could have been better."

Nevertheless, Comăneci had stolen the hearts of an international TV audience. She became an instant celebrity. Crowds flocked around her at public appearances. Everybody wanted a closer look at the girl who defined perfection in Montreal.

"I was so young," Comăneci said in 2012. "I didn't realize I was doing something no one had ever done, because I was doing the same routines I had always done, just in a bigger arena. People around me would say, 'That kid is so good,' but I thought adults just told kids they were good at something and patted them a little bit to make them feel good about themselves. I didn't know how good I was until I did what I did in Montreal."

Comăneci concluded her Olympic career at the 1980 Games in Moscow, Russia. She won two more gold medals there, but she tied for the silver medal in the all-around behind Yelena Davydova of the Soviet Union.

Nadia Comăneci performs on the balance beam at the 1976 Summer Games.

Nadia Comăneci scored the first perfect 10 in Olympics history on the uneven bars in the 1976 Summer Games.

Comăneci started in gymnastics at age six. She was one of the legendary Béla Károlyi's first students. Károlyi later coached Mary Lou Retton, who became the first US female gymnast to win the all-around title when she did so at the 1984 Games in Los Angeles. By then Comăneci had retired with a career total of nine Olympic medals.

Comăneci's perfect 10 can never be topped, though many gymnasts later tied her perfect score in the Olympics.

But since the 2004 Olympics in Athens, Greece, no athlete can join them. The international gymnastics federation changed the scoring system in 2006. Now scores are out of 20, and the best routines only score in the 16s. The goal was to eliminate controversy. However, many people still miss the simplicity of the perfect 10.

DREAM TEAM DOMINANCE

THE 1992 US OLYMPIC MEN'S BASKETBALL TEAM WAS CALLED THE "DREAM TEAM." THAT YEAR WAS THE FIRST TIME PROFESSIONAL BASKETBALL PLAYERS WERE ALLOWED TO PLAY IN THE OLYMPICS. THE US TEAM WAS STACKED WITH NATIONAL BASKETBALL ASSOCIATION ALL-STARS SUCH AS MICHAEL JORDAN, MAGIC JOHNSON, CHARLES BARKLEY, LARRY BIRD, PATRICK EWING, AND KARL MALONE. MANY PEOPLE WHO HAD NEVER FOLLOWED OLYMPIC BASKETBALL TUNED IN TO SEE THESE STARS. THEIR PLAY PROVED WORTHY OF THE ATTENTION.

THE DREAM TEAM SET MANY OLYMPIC RECORDS ON THE WAY TO WINNING THE GOLD MEDAL IN BARCELONA, SPAIN. IT WENT 8–0 AND WON BY AN AVERAGE MARGIN OF 43.8 POINTS. THE TEAM'S CLOSEST GAME WAS A 32-POINT WIN OVER CROATIA IN THE GOLD-MEDAL GAME. THE DREAM TEAM WAS SO GOOD THAT COACH CHUCK DALY NEVER CALLED A TIMEOUT DURING THE ENTIRE TOURNAMENT.

3

DOUBLE-
DOUBLE DIVER

Greg Louganis hugged his coach and cried. The record-setting US diver's emotions bubbled to the surface as he realized what he had accomplished. He also realized he was lucky to have been able to compete after a shocking accident.

Louganis had just swept the springboard and platform diving competitions at the 1988 Summer Games in Seoul, South Korea. He duplicated what he had done four years earlier, when he won the same two events at the 1984 Summer Games in Los Angeles.

Greg Louganis waves to the crowd after receiving the gold medal for platform diving at the 1988 Summer Games in Seoul, South Korea.

Never before had a male diver won both individual diving events in consecutive Olympics. In 1952 and 1956, Pat McCormick became the first female diver to do so. Besides McCormick and Louganis, no other diver has accomplished the double-double.

But the most amazing thing about Louganis's accomplishment in 1988 was that he was able to perform at all. He was leading the preliminaries of the 3-meter springboard—almost 10 feet above the water—in the ninth round as he prepared for his next dive. He was about to attempt a reverse 2 1/2 somersault in the pike position. That meant he leaped high into the air and performed two and a half back flips with his legs straight and pulled to his body. It was a difficult dive, but one he had done thousands of times before.

However, as Louganis leaped into the air, he failed to push far enough away from the springboard. As he completed his final somersault, the back of his head hit the diving board.

Louganis's body went limp as he fell into the water. It was a scary scene. He was able to climb out of the pool without any help, but he had a big cut on his head. Louganis returned 35 minutes later for his final two dives, with temporary stitches closing the wound on his head. He had fallen from first place to fifth after receiving a low score

Greg Louganis cracks his head against the diving board in the preliminaries of the 3-meter springboard competition at the 1988 Summer Games.

on the catastrophic dive. But that was the last thing on his mind.

"I didn't realize I was that close to the board," Louganis said of the accident. "When I hit it, it was kind of a shock. But I think my pride was hurt more than anything else."

Any diver would be excused for being nervous or hesitant at that point. But back on the board, Louganis performed another reverse somersault dive. This time his head cleared the board and he nailed the dive. He scored 87.12 points, the highest score by any diver in the preliminaries. After qualifying for the final round with his last dive, Louganis went to the hospital. Doctors closed the cut on his head with five stitches and applied a waterproof patch.

In the 3-meter finals the next day, Louganis put on a remarkable performance. He hit all of his dives, including the same one on which he was injured a day earlier. His courage and grace helped him win the gold medal.

A week later, Louganis won a repeat gold medal in the platform competition, becoming the first man to ever win consecutive golds in both events. Platform diving is staged on a solid platform 10 meters (almost 33 feet) above the water. And just like the springboard competition, the platform event was also filled with drama.

Greg Louganis is helped out of the water after hitting his head on the diving board at the 1988 Summer Games in Seoul, South Korea.

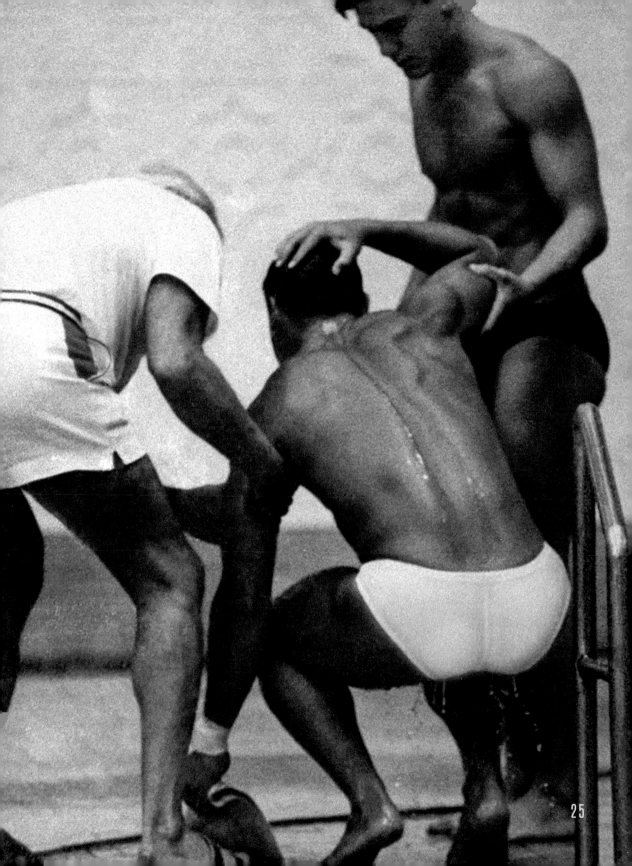

25

Greg Louganis competes in the platform diving finals at the 1988 Summer Games. He won the gold medal, becoming the first man to sweep the springboard and platform competitions at back-to-back Olympics.

Louganis was trailing 14-year-old Xiong Ni of China by three points with one dive remaining. Although Louganis— who was twice Xiong's age—did not perform his final dive perfectly, his dive had a higher degree of difficulty than Xiong's. That gave him the edge he needed to win the gold medal.

As remarkable as Louganis's feat was, he could have made it a triple-double if not for politics. At the 1976 Summer Olympics in Montreal, Canada, Louganis captured the silver medal on platform and took sixth in the springboard. He was just 16 with a bright future ahead of him.

He would have been a favorite in both events in the 1980 Summer Games in Moscow, Russia. However, the United States led a boycott of those Olympics to protest the Soviet Union's invasion of Afghanistan. Soviet Aleksandr Portnov won gold in the springboard and Falk Hoffmann of East Germany took gold in the platform. Louganis had to wait four more years before embarking on his historic journey.

HENIE'S THREE-PEAT

SONJA HENIE OF NORWAY WAS ONE OF THE MOST POPULAR MOVIE STARS OF HER ERA. BUT SHE WAS A RECORD-SETTING ATHLETE FIRST. HENIE IS THE ONLY FEMALE FIGURE SKATER TO WIN THREE OLYMPIC GOLD MEDALS IN THE SINGLES COMPETITION.

IN 1924 HENIE FINISHED IN EIGHTH PLACE AT HER FIRST OLYMPICS IN CHAMONIX, FRANCE. THAT WAS A PRETTY GOOD SHOWING, CONSIDERING SHE WAS ELEVEN YEARS OLD. SHE THEN WON CONSECUTIVE GOLDS AT ST. MORITZ, SWITZERLAND, IN 1928; LAKE PLACID, NEW YORK, IN 1932; AND GARMISCH-PARTENKIRCHEN, GERMANY, IN 1936.

HENIE'S GRACE AND ARTISTRY USHERED IN A NEW ERA FOR THE SPORT. AFTER SHE WON HER THIRD GOLD MEDAL AND TENTH STRAIGHT WORLD CHAMPIONSHIP, SHE RETIRED FROM COMPETITION. SHE WAS JUST 23. HENIE WENT TO HOLLYWOOD AND BECAME AN ACTRESS. SHE ALSO SKATED PROFESSIONALLY IN SHOWS FOR YEARS TO COME.

4
BRILLIANCE
ON THE BEACH

Misty May-Treanor and Kerri Walsh Jennings were not just the first beach volleyball superstars in the United States. They will be forever remembered as one of the best duos in Olympic history.

Beach volleyball had been added to the Olympics in 1996. May-Treanor and Walsh Jennings won their first gold medal together in the 2004 Summer Games in Athens, Greece. Then they won again four years later in Beijing, China. Their skills were a perfect match for each other. The 6-foot-3-inch (1.91-m) Walsh Jennings dominated at the net, while at 5 feet 9 (1.75 m), May-Treanor was a defensive dynamo on the back half of the court.

Kerri Walsh Jennings, *right*, sets a ball for teammate Misty May-Treanor during beach volleyball competition at the 2012 Summer Games in London, England.

They reunited for their third and final Olympics in 2012. But they had no idea how they would fare in London, England. In the previous four years, Walsh Jennings had given birth to two children—and was, in fact, five weeks pregnant with her third child when the London Games began. Meanwhile, just two months after the Beijing Olympics, May-Treanor ruptured her Achilles tendon while practicing for a performance on *Dancing with the Stars*. That injury to the back of her left ankle affected her ability to leap and move around. While May-Treanor recovered, Walsh Jennings played with a new partner.

They decided to take one more shot at Olympic gold in London. They also had one other goal: 21–0. That would be 21 matches without a loss. They were unbeaten in Athens in 2004 and again in Beijing in 2008. They wanted to see if they could do it again in London.

The competition setting for beach volleyball at the London Olympics was like a scene from a fairy tale. Sand was trucked in and laid down at the magnificent Horse Guards Parade in Westminster. Big Ben loomed on the skyline. It certainly looked nothing like a beach.

But the setting was not the only unfamiliar element for May-Treanor and Walsh Jennings. After winning their first two matches, they lost the first set of their next one against a team from Austria. It was the first time May-Treanor and

Misty May-Treanor bumps the ball at the 2012 Summer Games in London, England.

Walsh Jennings had lost a set at the Olympics. But after the 21–17 defeat in that first set, they stormed back to win the second 21–8. Then they took the third 15–10 to keep their streak alive.

"I was furious," Walsh Jennings told reporters after the match. "I want to go to the practice court and fix it."

The partners clearly figured out what had gone wrong. In the final, they defeated the other US team of April Ross and Jennifer Kessy 21–16, 21–16 to win the gold medal. And they did it their usual way, with May-Treanor's terrific defense and Walsh Jennings's tough play at the net.

"It's hard to stay on top," May-Treanor told reporters after their victory. "Winning the first gold medal, we were young, it was sweet. It was like, 'OK, we did it.' Winning back-to-back gold medals is very difficult. The target [on your back] is huge. To go for a three-peat, I don't know if you could write [it], the way it turned out."

After the final point of the gold-medal match, the two collapsed on the sand and gave each other a big hug. They accepted their opponents' congratulations, then took a victory lap around the court. Walsh Jennings scooped up her two young boys with an American flag draped around her.

"I didn't plan [it], but I'm really glad we could share that minute," Walsh Jennings said.

Misty May-Treanor, *left*, and Kerri Walsh Jennings celebrate their victory in the gold-medal match at the 2012 Summer Games.

Misty May-Treanor, *left*, and Kerri Walsh Jennings show off their record third gold medals in beach volleyball, won at the 2012 Summer Games in London, England.

May-Treanor and Walsh Jennings were teammates for 11 years. How did they maintain their partnership? They said they were as close as sisters, from the beginning all the way until the end.

"Above all, I'm just really proud to finish the journey with Misty how we finished it." Walsh Jennings said.

HEIDEN'S DRIVE FOR FIVE

US SPEED SKATER ERIC HEIDEN DELIVERED ONE OF THE GREATEST PERFORMANCES IN HISTORY AT THE 1980 OLYMPIC WINTER GAMES IN LAKE PLACID, NEW YORK. HEIDEN SWEPT ALL FIVE LONG-TRACK SPEED SKATING EVENTS, MAKING HIM THE FIRST PERSON TO WIN FIVE INDIVIDUAL GOLD MEDALS IN THE SAME OLYMPICS. AND HE DID IT IN A SPAN OF NINE DAYS.

ALL TOLD, HEIDEN SET FOUR OLYMPIC RECORDS AND ONE WORLD RECORD. THE NIGHT BEFORE WINNING HIS FIFTH GOLD, HEIDEN WATCHED THE US MEN'S HOCKEY TEAM DEFEAT THE SOVIET UNION IN A GAME THAT BECAME KNOWN AS "THE MIRACLE ON ICE." ONE COULD ARGUE THAT HEIDEN PROVIDED A MIRACLE OF HIS OWN IN LAKE PLACID.

5

MAKING A SPLASH

Nothing is impossible. That was Michael Phelps's message after he won his record eighth gold medal at the 2008 Summer Games in Beijing, China. He had already competed in two Olympics and won eight medals—six of them gold—before Beijing. His performance in the Chinese capital confirmed that he was the greatest Olympic swimmer of all time.

Fellow American swimmer Mark Spitz had won seven gold medals at the 1972 Olympics in Munich, West Germany. Never before had anyone earned more first-place finishes at a single Olympic Games. Breaking Spitz's record was no easy task.

US swimmer Michael Phelps is the most decorated Olympian of all time.

Probably the most thrilling individual race for Phelps in Beijing was the gold he won in the 100-meter butterfly. He came from behind to beat Milorad Čavić, literally by a fingertip. It was the only race in which Phelps did not set a world record. But what he did to reach the wall was amazing. Phelps managed to squeeze in a quick half-stroke to touch the wall first. He won by one hundredth of a second—50.58 seconds to 50.59 seconds.

Five of Phelps's gold medals came in individual events. His eighth and final event was the 400-meter medley relay. Phelps was swimming the third of the four legs. When he dived into the water, Phelps and his American teammates were trailing mighty Australia. But Phelps powered into the lead on his return lap. That left it up to anchor Jason Lezak to bring it home. Lezak did just that. Phelps's eighth gold medal was assured.

"I don't even know what to feel right now," Phelps told reporters at the swimming arena, known to fans as the Water Cube. "There's so much emotions going through my head and so much excitement. I kind of just want to see my mom."

Phelps's mother, Debbie, was in the stands with her two daughters watching the record performance. She was proud and happy.

Michael Phelps reacts to his razor-thin victory over Milorad Čavić, *left*, in the 100-meter butterfly finals at the 2008 Summer Games in Beijing, China.

"Nothing is impossible," Michael Phelps said. "With so many people saying it couldn't be done, all it takes is an imagination, and that's something I learned and something that helped me."

Phelps's six other gold medals came in the 400 individual medley, 200 butterfly, 200 freestyle, 200 individual medley, 800 freestyle relay, and 400 freestyle relay.

Four years later at the 2012 Summer Games in London, Phelps competed in his fourth Olympics and added to his career-record total. He won four more gold medals and two silvers. He ended the meet as the most successful swimmer for the third Olympics in a row.

Phelps's final event was the 400 medley relay, just as it was in Beijing. He again helped the United States win the race. The gold was the eighteenth of his career and his twenty-second medal overall.

After Phelps's last event, the International Swimming Federation honored him with a trophy as the most decorated Olympian ever. He surpassed Soviet gymnast Larisa Latynina, who won 18 medals—including nine golds—between 1956 and 1964.

Phelps started swimming at age seven. The Maryland native took to the sport in part because his older sisters swam. He was a very active child, and his mom wanted him

Michael Phelps hoists the trophy recognizing him as the most decorated Olympian ever. He won 22 medals, 18 of them gold, in Athens, Beijing, and London.

41

Living true to his motto, nothing was impossible when Michael Phelps entered the pool.

to participate in a sport that would help him concentrate. He was so good that he was setting national swimming records for his age group by age 10.

Five years later, he qualified for the 2000 Summer Olympics in Sydney, Australia, at age 15. That made him the youngest swimming Olympian in 68 years. He did not win a medal in Sydney. But he was proud that he made the finals in the 200 butterfly. His fifth-place showing in that race provided just a hint of what was to come.

BIATHLON BRILLIANCE

OLE EINAR BJØRNDALEN WAS CALLED KING OF BIATHLON—A SPORT THAT COMBINES CROSS-COUNTRY SKIING AND RIFLE SHOOTING—LONG BEFORE HE BECAME THE MOST DECORATED ATHLETE IN WINTER OLYMPICS HISTORY. THE NORWEGIAN WON 13 MEDALS IN SIX OLYMPICS. HIS LAST CAME IN 2014 IN SOCHI, RUSSIA, AT AGE 40. BJØRNDALEN HAS A TOTAL OF EIGHT OLYMPIC GOLD MEDALS, FOUR SILVERS, AND ONE BRONZE. HE RETIRED IN 2014 AFTER HELPING NORWAY WIN THE FIRST OLYMPIC MIXED RELAY IN BIATHLON.

FUN FACTS

KID DIVER

When Marjorie Gestring, *below*, took first in springboard diving at the 1936 Olympics in Berlin, Germany, she became the world's youngest Summer Olympic gold medalist. The US diver was only 13 years, 268 days old.

MULTIPLE MEDALS

Philip Noel-Baker of England won a silver medal in the men's 1,500-meter run at the 1920 Olympic Games in Antwerp, Belgium. But his greatest accomplishment came many years later. In 1959 Noel-Baker won the Nobel Peace Prize. He was the first Olympian to accomplish the honor.

SENIOR SHOOTER

Oscar Swahn of Sweden was considered the "old man" of his Swedish team when he won three Olympic medals in shooting at age 60 at the 1908 Olympics. Twelve years later, Swahn returned after serving in World War I and helped his country win the silver medal in the running deer double-shot team event at the 1920 Olympics. He was 72. Swahn remains the oldest Olympian ever.

FABULOUS FLOP

Dick Fosbury, *below*, won the 1968 Olympic gold medal in the high jump by becoming the first athlete to leap backward over the bar. He invented the technique, called the Fosbury Flop, in high school. It is still used by high jumpers today. His gold-medal winning leap was 7 feet, 4 1/4 inches (2.24 m).

GLOSSARY

anchor
The last swimmer in a relay race.

boycott
When a group of people refuse to buy a product or participate in an event.

butterfly
One of the most difficult strokes in swimming, in which both arms stroke simultaneously as the legs kick together.

dismount
When the gymnast gets off an apparatus or completes a floor exercise, typically landing on both feet.

foul
In the long jump, when an athlete's toe or foot crosses the takeoff line illegally.

heptathlon
A women's track-and-field event in which the competitors participate in seven events—the 100-meter hurdles, high jump, shot put, 200-meter dash, long jump, javelin throw, and 800-meter run—over two days to determine a winner.

long-track course
A 400-meter (437-yard) oval used in speed skating.

uneven bars
An event in women's gymnastics featuring two parallel bars set at different heights.

FOR MORE INFORMATION

Peters, Stephanie True. *Great Moments in the Summer Olympics.* New York: Little, Brown and Co., 2012.

Rosen, Karen. *Great Moments in Olympic Track & Field.* Minneapolis, MN: Abdo Publishing, 2014.

Wallechinsky, David and Jaime Loucky. *The Complete Book of the Olympics.* London: Aurum, 2012.

WEBSITES

To learn more about Record Breakers, visit **booklinks.abdopublishing.com**. These links are routinely monitored and updated to provide the most current information available.

PLACE TO VISIT

US Olympic Training Center
1750 E. Boulder St.
Colorado Springs, Colorado 80909
(719) 866-4618
www.teamusa.org
The US Olympic team has welcomed millions of visitors to its headquarters in Colorado Springs, Colorado. In addition to extensive training facilities for elite athletes, the USOTC offers visitors the chance to discover US Olympic history through its indoor and outdoor exhibitions. Walking tours are conducted daily.

INDEX

Barkley, Charles, 19
Beamon, Bob, 4, 6–8, 10–11
Beer, Klaus, 10
Bird, Larry, 19
Bjørndalen, Ole Einar, 43
Boston, Ralph, 4, 6–8, 11

Čavić, Milorad, 39
Comăneci, Nadia, 12, 14, 17–18

Daly, Chuck, 19
Davies, Lynn, 7
Davydova, Yelena, 17

Ewing, Patrick, 19

Heiden, Eric, 35

Henie, Sonja, 27
Hoffmann, Falk, 27

Johnson, Magic, 69
Jordan, Michael, 19
Joyner-Kersee, Jackie, 11

Károlyi, Béla, 18
Kessy, Jennifer, 32

Latynina, Larisa, 40
Lezak, Jason, 39
Louganis, Greg, 20, 23–24, 26–27

Malone, Karl, 19
May-Treanor, Misty, 28, 31–32, 34–35
McCormick, Pat, 23

Ni, Xiong, 26

Owens, Jesse, 10

Phelps, Debbie, 39
Phelps, Michael, 36, 39–40, 42–43
Portnov, Aleksandr, 27
Powell, Mike, 11

Retton, Mary Lou, 18
Ross, April, 32

Spitz, Mark, 36

Ter-Ovanesyan, Igor, 7

Walsh Jennings, Kerri, 28, 31–32, 34–35

ABOUT THE AUTHOR

Award-winning journalist Jo-Ann Barnas has traveled to more than a dozen countries writing about international sporting events, including eight Olympic Games. She worked for the *Detroit Free Press* from 1995 to 2012. She was voted 2005 Michigan Sportswriter of the Year by the National Sportscasters and Sportswriters Association. Other top honors include two national first-place APSE awards. Barnas began her professional career in 1984 at the *Kansas City Star.*